EARTH SCIENCE–OUR PLANET Need to Know

SilverTip

The Atmosphere

by D. R. Faust
Consultant: Jordan Stoleru, Science Educator

Minneapolis, Minnesota

Credits
Cover and title page, © buradaki/Shutterstock; 3, © desertsolitaire/Shutterstock; 5, © Pinglabel/Shutterstock; 7, © Dani Jara/Shutterstock; 9, © FoxGrafy/Shutterstock; 10–11, © Public Domain/NASA; 13, © Shanti Hesse/Shutterstock; 14–15, © Gina Hendrick/Shutterstock; 17, © Sakurra/iStock; 19, © PaulFleet/iStock; 21, © Dennis MacDonald/Shutterstock; 22–23, © Gatien GREGORI/Shutterstock; 25, © BEST-BACKGROUNDS/Shutterstock; 27, © DC Studio/Shutterstock; 28, © Macrovector/Shutterstock.

Bearport Publishing Company Product Development Team
Publisher: Jen Jenson; Director of Product Development: Spencer Brinker; Editorial Director: Allison Juda; Editor: Cole Nelson; Editor: Tiana Tran; Production Editor: Naomi Reich; Art Director: Kim Jones; Designer: Kayla Eggert; Designer: Steve Scheluchin; Production Specialist: Owen Hamlin

Statement on Usage of Generative Artificial Intelligence
Bearport Publishing remains committed to publishing high-quality nonfiction books. Therefore, we restrict the use of generative AI to ensure accuracy of all text and visual components pertaining to a book's subject. See BearportPublishing.com for details.

Library of Congress Cataloging-in-Publication Data is available at www.loc.gov or upon request from the publisher.

ISBN: 979-8-89577-067-2 (hardcover)
ISBN: 979-8-89577-514-1 (paperback)
ISBN: 979-8-89577-184-6 (ebook)

Copyright © 2026 Bearport Publishing Company. All rights reserved. No part of this publication may be reproduced in whole or in part, stored in any retrieval system, or transmitted in any form or by any means, electronic, mechanical, photocopying, recording, or otherwise, without written permission from the publisher. Bearport Publishing is a division of FlutterBee Education Group.

For more information, write to Bearport Publishing, 3500 American Blvd W, Suite 150, Bloomington, MN 55431.

Contents

An Invisible Blanket 4
Getting Gassy 6
Lovely Layers 8
At Home in the Troposphere 12
Block It Out 16
Burning Up 18
Human Harm 20
Wild Weather 24
Keep It Clean 26

Layers of the Atmosphere 28
SilverTips for Success 29
Glossary 30
Read More 31
Learn More Online 31
Index 32
About the Author 32

An Invisible Blanket

Earth is surrounded by an invisible blanket. The planet is wrapped in layers of gas called the atmosphere (AT-muh-*sfeer*). Even though you can't see it, Earth's atmosphere is key to life on our planet.

Earth is not the only planet surrounded by gases. Every planet in our solar system except Mercury has some kind of atmosphere. However, Earth's is the only one that supports life.

Getting Gassy

The atmosphere is made up of a mix of gases. More than 70 percent of it is nitrogen. There is also a lot of oxygen and **carbon dioxide**. Small amounts of hydrogen, **methane**, and other gases are mixed in, too.

> Earth's atmosphere holds some solids. Dust and ash from volcanoes and wildfires can get thrown into the sky. Sometimes, they are swept up by strong winds. They join the gases of the atmosphere.

Lovely Layers

Earth's atmosphere has five layers. The troposphere (TROH-poh-*sfeer*) is closest to Earth. The highest layer is the exosphere (EG-zoh-*sfeer*). It reaches up to 6,200 miles (10,000 km) above the ground. In between are the stratosphere (STRAT-uh-*sfeer*), mesosphere (MEZ-oh-*sfeer*), and thermosphere (THER-moh-*sfeer*).

Most humans live in the troposphere. But astronauts on the International Space Station are in the thermosphere. This is the second-farthest layer of the atmosphere from Earth.

Earth's Atmosphere

Exosphere

Thermosphere

Mesosphere

Stratosphere

Troposphere

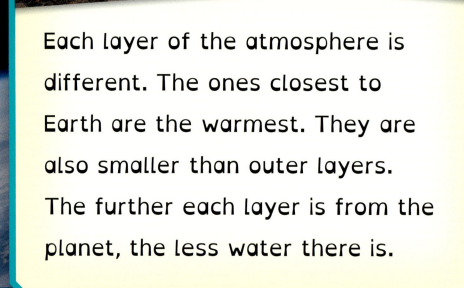

Each layer of the atmosphere is different. The ones closest to Earth are the warmest. They are also smaller than outer layers. The further each layer is from the planet, the less water there is.

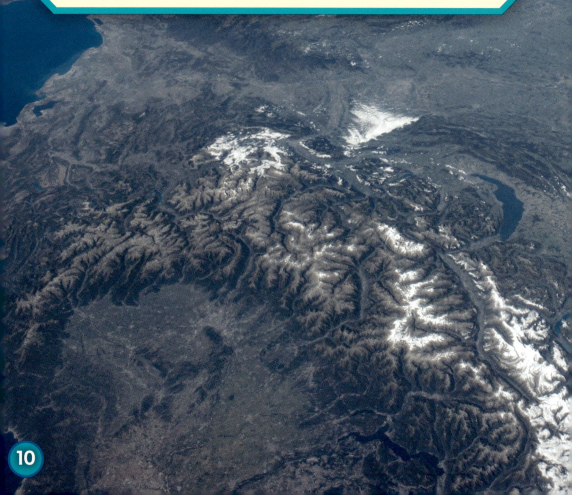

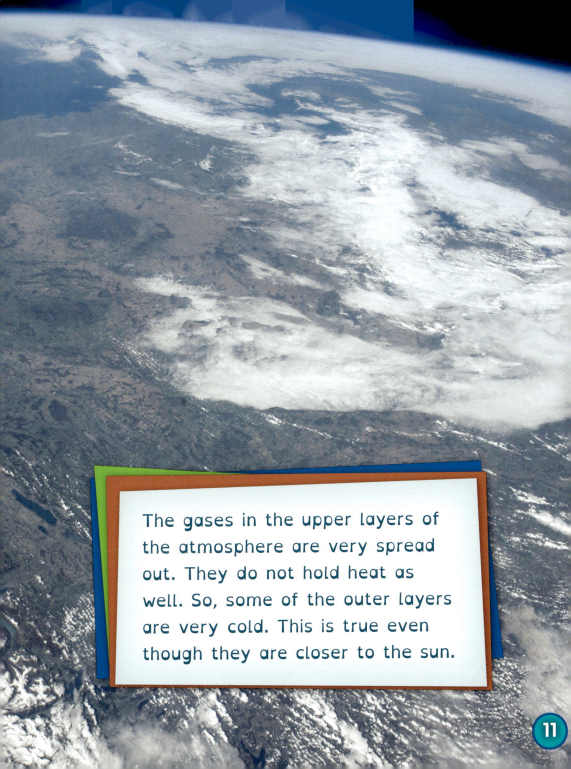

The gases in the upper layers of the atmosphere are very spread out. They do not hold heat as well. So, some of the outer layers are very cold. This is true even though they are closer to the sun.

At Home in the Troposphere

The troposphere is the only layer of the atmosphere that readily supports life. Its gases keep the planet warm. It also has enough oxygen for animals and carbon dioxide for plants. This layer holds in water that all living things need.

> Plants and animals exchange oxygen and carbon dioxide. Animals use oxygen to create energy. They breathe out carbon dioxide. Plants take in carbon dioxide to make energy and release oxygen.

Most of Earth's weather happens in the troposphere, too. Weather is formed by warm and cold air moving around in the atmosphere. We feel the air move as wind. This wind carries rain clouds and water **vapor** around the planet. Storms can form where warm and cold air meet.

Water vapor in the air gathers into clouds. Over time, clouds fill up with this water. They let it out as rain or snow.

Block It Out

The layers above the troposphere help protect life on Earth. Energy from the sun keeps the planet warm. However, it can also be harmful. The sun lets out dangerous **radiation** energy. Luckily, the stratosphere has the **ozone layer**. This layer of oxygen stops most of the sun's radiation.

> Radiation from sunlight can damage our skin. A small amount can cause skin to get darker. Too much can lead to a sunburn.

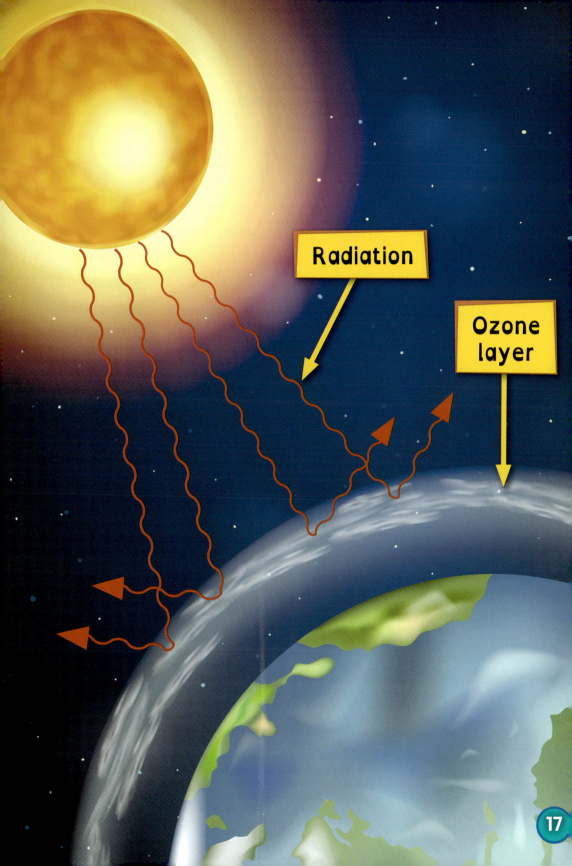

Burning Up

The mesopshere also protects us from space-based dangers. **Meteors** are large space rocks. Sometimes, they head toward Earth. If they made it to Earth's surface, they could cause harm. Fortunately, most meteors burn up in the gases of the mesosphere.

> Some meteors make it through the atmosphere and hit the planet. Then they are called meteorites. The largest one ever found is 9 feet (2.7 m) across.

What we call shooting stars are actually meteors burning up.

Human Harm

The mix of gases in the atmosphere keeps Earth warm enough for life to exist. But humans are changing that balance. We burn **fossil fuels** for power. This power heats our homes, runs our cars, and fuels our factories. But when we burn these fuels, it also adds more gases to the atmosphere.

> Fossil fuels include gasoline, coal, and natural gas. They are made out of the remains of plants and animals that died millions of years ago.

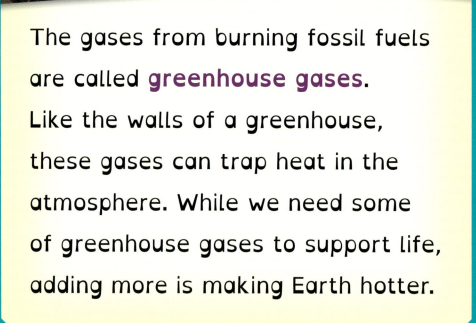

The gases from burning fossil fuels are called **greenhouse gases**. Like the walls of a greenhouse, these gases can trap heat in the atmosphere. While we need some of greenhouse gases to support life, adding more is making Earth hotter.

Carbon dioxide and methane are greenhouse gases. Smoke from factories and cars adds carbon dioxide to the atmosphere. Cows make methane in their stomachs and burp it out.

Wild Weather

A hotter atmosphere can be harmful to life on Earth. Even a few degrees of warming can change weather around the world. It can make some places drier, leading to **droughts**. Other places may get more rain, leading to floods.

> A warmer atmosphere heats the ocean up, too. This can lead to stronger **hurricanes**. These storms may also last much longer.

Keep It Clean

The atmosphere protects Earth. The best thing we can do for life on the planet is to keep the air around us clean. We can use fewer fossil fuels to reduce greenhouse gases and slow warming. Keeping our atmosphere healthy will help keep life on Earth healthy, too.

Planting trees also helps the atmosphere. Trees take in the greenhouse gas carbon dioxide. They also let out the oxygen we need to breathe.

Layers of the Atmosphere

The five layers of the atmosphere all help protect life on Earth. Some layers make our weather. Other layers block objects from space.

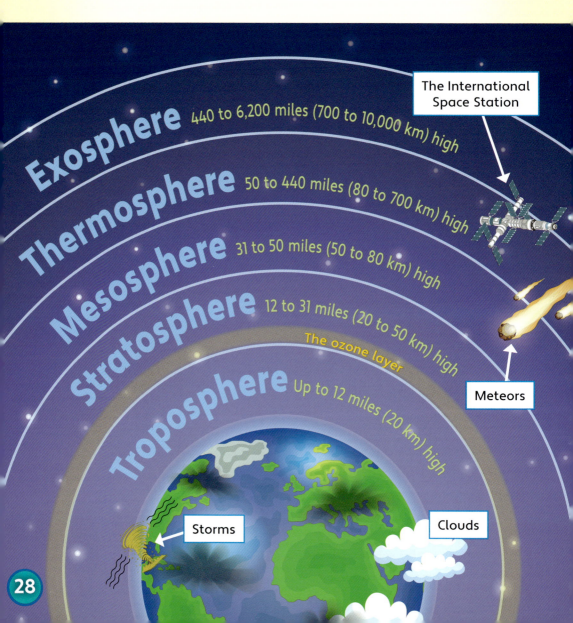

SilverTips for SUCCESS

★ SilverTips for REVIEW

Review what you've learned. Use the text to help you.

Define key terms

greenhouse gases
ozone layer
radiation
troposphere
weather

Check for understanding

How many layers does Earth's atmosphere have? Name three of them.

Describe one way the atmosphere supports life on Earth.

What are greenhouse gases?

Think deeper

How would changes in the atmosphere affect your life on Earth?

★ SilverTips on TEST-TAKING

- **Make a study plan.** Ask your teacher what the test is going to cover. Then, set aside time to study a little bit every day.

- **Read all the questions carefully.** Be sure you know what is being asked.

- **Skip any questions** you don't know how to answer right away. Mark them and come back later if you have time.

Glossary

carbon dioxide a greenhouse gas given off when animals breathe or fossil fuels are burned

droughts long periods with little to no rain

fossil fuels natural gas, coal, and oil formed from plant or animal remains

greenhouse gases the gases that trap the sun's heat around Earth

hurricanes large, powerful, and destructive storms with very strong winds

meteors chunks of rock or metal that fall from space and burn up in Earth's atmosphere

methane a greenhouse gas that is made by livestock or released from underground mines and caves

ozone layer a layer of gas in Earth's atmosphere that stops some of the sun's radiation from reaching Earth's surface

radiation a dangerous form of energy that moves in invisible waves or rays

vapor water in a gas form

Read More

McMichael, Karen. *The Atmosphere (The Inside Guide: Earth's Four Spheres).* New York: Cavendish Square, 2023.

Wargula, Doris. *Earth's Atmosphere (Discover More! A Look at Weather and Climate).* Buffalo: Britannica Educational Publishing, 2025.

Woolf, Alex, and Steve Evans. *Atmosphere and Weather (Building Blocks of Geography).* Chicago: World Book, 2023.

Learn More Online

1. Go to **FactSurfer.com** or scan the QR code below.
2. Enter "**The Atmosphere**" into the search box.
3. Click on the cover of this book to see a list of websites.

Index

carbon dioxide 6, 12, 22, 26

clouds 14–15, 28

exosphere 8–9, 28

fossil fuels 20, 22, 26

greenhouse gases 22, 26

hurricanes 24

mesosphere 8–9, 18, 28

meteors 18-19, 28

oxygen 6, 8, 12, 16, 26

ozone layer 16–17, 28

radiation 16–17

sun, the 11, 16

troposphere 8–9, 12, 14, 16, 28

About the Author

D. R. Faust is a freelance writer of fiction and nonfiction. They live in Queens, NY.